Old Dogs

lessons in loving & ageing

SUZANNE MCCOURT

PHOTOGRAPHS BY PETER DERRETT

POSH DOG PUBLISHING

National Library of Australia
Cataloguing-in-Publication Entry

McCourt, Suzanne.
Old dogs: lessons in loving and ageing /by Suzanne McCourt;
photographs by Peter Derrett.

p. cm.
ISBN 978 0 9873775 0 0

    1. Dogs – humor.
    2. Dogs – inspiration.
    3. Dogs – pictorial works
    4. Photography of dogs

Book design by Damian Grant
Manufactured by Everbest in China
Published by Posh Dog Publishing

For further information about orders:
Email: orders@dogablog.com.au
Website: www.dogablog.com.au

For Brando
(of course)
and dog lovers all over the world.

IN THE BEGINNING

He came romping towards me that day on the pier like a big brown bear with dreadlocks hanging almost down to the ground.

'What a magnificent creature!' I said.

'He is,' said the owner, 'but I have to find him a new home.'

'I'll have him!' I said. And that's how it all began.

He was a three year old Poodle named Bran after the mythical Irish god of the sea. It was a very good name for a dog who loved swimming but when our children saw how besotted and just plain silly we were with him they called him *All-Bran*. 'No way!' we said and he became Brando with absolutely no connection to method–acting Marlon except for being the big star of our lives.

Brando was with us through all the happy times and hard times that come with second marriages and blended families and if he was sometimes wild and disobedient that was probably around the time my mother died and he needed a firm hand

and I was grieving too much to be firm with anyone, especially him. And every morning he would swim far out to sea with his father, blue bathing cap and black poodle perm becoming smaller and smaller until they turned at the marker and swam back to shore. And in no time at all he became a hospital therapy dog and visited Aids patients and the elderly and once a nurse lifted him onto the bed of a tiny old lady who almost died of excitement and we didn't do that again.

When my grandson was born, he rode Brando like a horse and later dressed him in fairy dresses and tinsel and Christmas ribbons. We built forts and made him the baddie and locked him outside but he just waited patiently until the grandson went home and life could return to normal except for food droppings on the floor which were always much better when the grandson was around.

For such a big dog, Brando was the gentlest of giants. His eyes seemed to carry the wisdom of the whole world, almost as if his old soul and had been here many times before. He was regal and wise, funny and kind, and mostly we took him for granted and forgot that life always comes to an end—for dogs and for all of us—and how scary is that? But slowly and surely he became an old dog with stiff legs and grey hair and strange lumpy protuberances. He grew hard of hearing and lost interest in the ginger cat down the street that had excited him for years. Yet his big heart stayed brave and true: a publisher's rejection guaranteed a thorough face-licking: dogs passing the house, still earned a croaky rebuke.

Then one day we looked into his poor suffering eyes and knew the time had come. We helped him into the car and drove twice round the roundabout on the way to the vet, delaying, weeping. At the hospital we stroked his fluffy ears and cried and watched him slip gently into bliss. When he was gone, the grief was unbearable. Yet we knew without a doubt that he had come to us that day on the pier for a season and for a reason. He had come to teach us the important things about living and dying that can only be learned by loving and being loved in return.

I know you have shared the same journey as me. This book is for you and your beloved old dogs, and for Brando too.

Old Dogs

lessons in loving & ageing

OLD DOGS
teach us new tricks
like how to throw sticks
and FETCH them
OURSELVES.

More surprisingly
they teach us how to
NOSE GROINS with IMPUNITY.

And how to
dawdle at the lights
while contemplating
CYCLISTS in LYCRA
and their
TIGHT ROUND BOTTOMS.

IT IS ALSO
worth considering
how they teach us to
become more DISCERNING
about who we let into our lives.

GENERALLY, old friends who
know how to find the ITCHY SPOT
are more welcome than those who
like the sound of their own voice
and don't know when to leave.

More importantly
they teach us PATIENCE
which is a DOGLY VIRTUE
inspired by a Dog called Job
who remained steadfast through
disasters and was BLESSED.

And they teach
FORBEARANCE
which is similar to patience
but involves a lot of WAITING

WAITING for them to come home.

Waiting for the fridge to open.

Waiting for a walk.

Waiting to meet the DOGLY MAKER.

Waiting. Waiting.

And they teach us GRATITUDE
for small things. A warm bed. A wet kiss.
Those heaters outside coffee shops
that warm the pavement
on cold days..

...also PLUM JAM DONUTS!

Consider also how they
teach us COURAGE.

Despite every kind of ACHE and PAIN
still they kick up wobbly legs
and bunny bounce after balls.

See that FLASH of JOY!
They are so brave.
Every day.
In every way.

Furthermore,
they are LOYAL, they are TRUE,
they are wonderful
at LICKING WOUNDS.

They are tuned
to reading LONELY MINDS.
They are ALWAYS THERE
next to the fire, the phone,
the bed, the chair.

JUST THERE!

Let's not forget BLIND DOGS
and GUIDE DOGS!

They deserve MEDALS
for negotiating life in their
BRAVE and TRUSTING way.

Old Dogs are also very ZEN.
They understand the importance of
TAKING LOTS of NAPS.

(Except when the doorbell rings.)

Old Dogs understand
the pleasure of
LIFE'S SIMPLE THINGS.

A MEATY BONE...
A GOOD DIG...

...the BLISS of a
COOL BREEZE blowing
through long fluffy ears.

Some old dogs develop
SECOND SIGHT.

This is why they sleep
with OPEN EYES.

They are MEDITATING
on days gone by,
on liver drops
and carob frogs...

...on the way SUNLIGHT
streams through
a windowpane
and turns a grey morning
into a ROSY DAY.

Some old dogs remain
FOLLOWERS of FASHION.

Some DON'T!

Sometimes

keeping up appearances

can become

LIFE'S GREATEST CHALLENGE.

Some
take this to
EXTREMES!

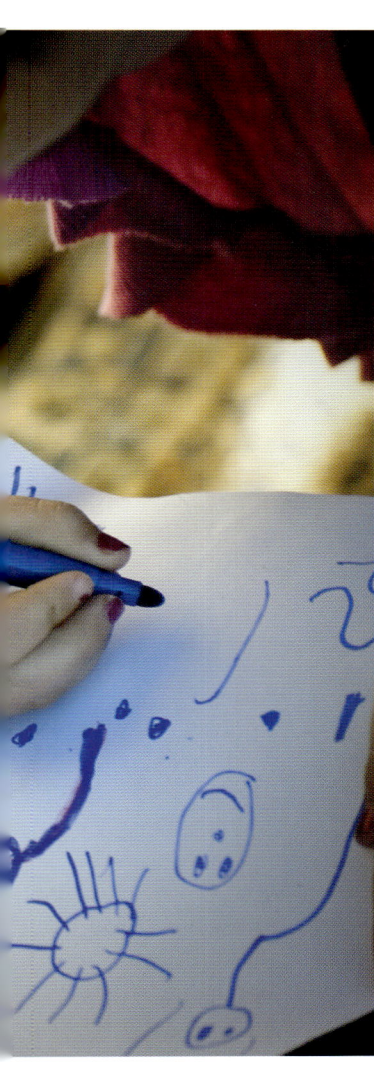

Others have
their minds on
HIGHER THINGS.

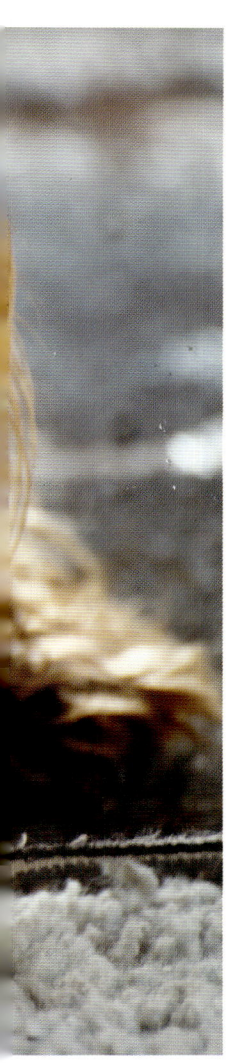

Some remain OLD WARRIORS
ever ready with a warning growl
and a foolish eagerness to
stand their ground.

This can involve a lot of
HUFF and PUFF
and STRUTTING of their STUFF.

Some old dogs become
a little GRUMPY.

Some old dogs even know
when it's TIME TO GO!

We know of one old dog
who DUG HIS OWN HOLE!
(and he never was a digging dog!)
How ASTONISHING is that?
How WONDERFUL!
How SAD.

Dare we mention
the BIG 'E' word?

(Euthanasia)

Old dogs know
it is always waiting there.
TO BE OR NOT TO BE?
That is the question hanging
over their old heads.

What a minefield!
What a choice!

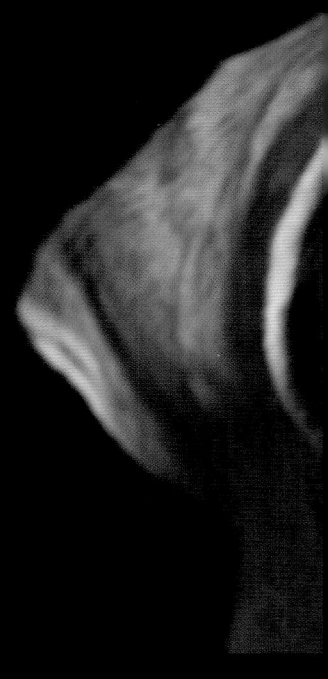

BUT TO GET TO THE POINT.

Despite the current VOGUE
for makeovers of every kind
old dogs teach us that
GREY hair, DROOPY jowls
and strange LUMPY protuberances
DO NOT of themselves turn
a silk purse into a sow's ear.

In a word, they teach us WISDOM
which is another DOGLY VIRTUE
documented by a dog called SOLOMON
who knew that a good strong heart
ALWAYS SHINES TRUE and
beneath the surface we remain forever
SVELTE YOUNG PUPPIES.

But maybe not!

Maybe that depends on the old

NATURE versus NURTURE debate.

LET'S NOT GO THERE!

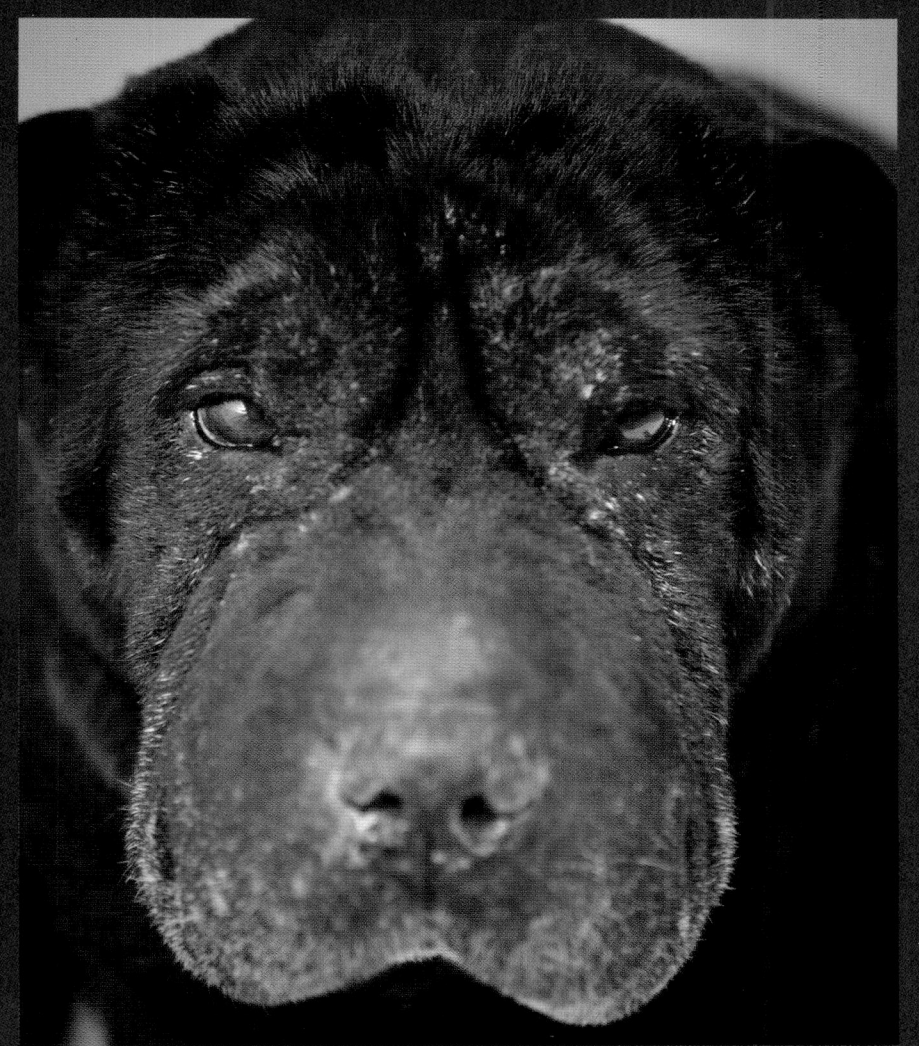

Yet WITHOUT A DOUBT
their greatest gift is LOVE
which is a LAW of DOGS
and IRREFUTABLE.

Not the SOPPY kind inspired by
tight bottoms, but the long lasting kind
that involves STICKING AROUND
through TOUGH TIMES and
DIGGING DEEP for bones.

For it is NO SECRET
that old dogs are really
ANGELS of a HAIRY KIND
sent to guide us to
THE OTHER SIDE.

Take a look at
ONE or TWO or TEN.
WITHOUT EXCEPTION
you will see it
IN THEIR EYES.

LOVE.

That's all there is.

THE END

SUZANNE McCOURT

After a career in teaching, marketing, public relations and private employment, Suzanne McCourt has embraced the joys and challenges of a writing life. Her first novel is currently with a publisher, she has won prizes for her short stories, and several of her poems trundle around Melbourne on trains as part of the Moving Galleries project.

Suzanne's life changed dramatically when she adopted Brando, a three year old Poodle of great gentleness and wisdom. Through Brando she became involved in pet therapy in hospitals and also founded FIDO & CO (Fellowship of Informed Dog Owners & Cat Owners), a community group that worked with her local Council to develop a Domestic Animal Plan which has made the Bayside area where she lives in suburban Melbourne, one of the most pet friendly in the world.

When Brando died, Suzanne discovered she was far from alone in loving and losing an old dog. She has written *'Old Dogs'* in remembrance of Brando and for dog owners all over the world.

PETER DERRETT OAM

Peter Derrett has been involved in teaching, theatre direction and photography all his life. He lives in Northern NSW and documents community events, festivals, dance and theatre. He has had extensive experience teaching Drama and Theatre and co-founded regional theatre company, *Theatre North,* with his wife Ros. His work was acknowledged in 2007 by an OAM award for services to Drama Education and Regional Theatre.

He and Ros have travelled widely and have written and photographed overseas. Peter has an exhibition on Venice in 2012. He won the Australasian Fine Art Photography Award at Monash University Gallery in 1998. His work has been published in national magazines and newspapers.

Peter has always photographed dogs. They are 'of the moment' and have wonderful personalities. This project has been very moving as it has brought him into contact with old dogs and their memorable owners. It has been a humbling experience. He expects further encounters with the canine kingdom.

ACKNOWLEDGEMENTS

To beautiful Brando who was inspiration and guide for this book and who taught us all he knew about loving and ageing. To our partners; Dr Ros Derrett, OAM, who has been there every step of the way for Peter with love and support, and a huge love of dogs; and to Stan Rankin, whose love and encouragement has enabled Suzanne to pursue her creative dreams.

Our deepest appreciation to Gillian Barnett who started the whole process by introducing friend to friend, and to her partner Ron Breth. To the ever patient Damian for working on every whim with such professionalism. To Jon Paterson and staff at the New Camera House, Lismore. To Genevera Hooper and the Eltham Village Gallery, Northern NSW. To Dianne Kors for sending us so many lovely old dogs. To Jeremy and staff at the Bayside Veterinary Clinic for helping find others.

To the many dog owners in the Bayside area of Melbourne, Victoria, and on the North Coast of New South Wales who have embraced this project and given of their time and beloved companions. For your generosity and support we thank you. May your old dogs live on forever in these pages.

THANK YOU

Chai & Rod • Lucy & Pete • Bear & Joan

Lily & Alana • John & Peter • Max & Sarah

Bob & Robin • Jonty & Peter • Oscar & Trish

Figgy & Noey • Beau & Diane • Duffy & Carly

Ellie & Pam and Tony • Brodie & Janet and Paul

Suzie & Meena • Gemma & Alan • Snowi and Jade

Ruby & Donna • Rupert & Gaye • Minya & Alison

Cookie & Erika • Cassie & Tracey • Kai & Margaret

Jimmy & Wendy • Lionel & Charles • Dakota & Debra

Sally & Christine • Princess & Danni • Santana & Janine

Conor & Lorraine • Vinnie & Rachael • Mambo & Glenċa

Morpheus & Mark • Samson & Natalie • Vicky & Sheenagh

Lily & Ginger and Rosemarie • Cowboy & Genevera and Lesley

Amos & Clarice and Gillian and Rob • Seb & Jo • Ned

SEE MORE OLD DOGS AT

www.dogablog.com.au